The Loneliness Paradox

Unveiling the Epidemic Shaping Your Life

By Lulu Anglebird

The Loneliness Paradox

Publisher:
Publisher Name: Draft2digital
Address: O Box 2860, Broken Arrow, OK 74013
Email: support@draft2digital.com
Phone: (866) 358-6413

Cover design is Designed by Lulu Anglebird.
Illustrations by Lulu Anglebird
Printed in Oklahoma City, Oklahoma

Disclaimer

This work is created with the permission of the people who volunteered to be a part of this book mixed with the life experiences of the author. This book might contain content that might be distressing for some users or spike back memories from their past.

Chapter 1
The Ghost in the Room
When Loneliness Wears a Crowd's Face

The rooftop bar was alive with the hum of conversation, the kind of place where laughter danced on the edges of wine glasses and the warm glow of string lights bathed everyone in a golden hue. From the outside, it was a picture-perfect scene of connection. You were there too, smiling at a coworker's joke, nodding along as a friend recounted their weekend, your Instagram story a carefully curated snapshot of belonging. But beneath the surface, a quiet, insidious truth gnawed at you: *No one here knows you. Not really.

You were an actor in a play, reciting lines, performing a version of yourself you thought the world would tolerate. The loneliest moment wasn't when you were physically alone—it was when you were surrounded by voices and realized yours had been muted.

This is the Loneliness Paradox: the sharper the ache of disconnection, the more desperately we cling to facades, believing *performance* is the price of belonging. But what happens when the mask becomes your face?

The Mask That Grafts to Your Skin

Loneliness isn't just solitude; it's the exhausting calculus of editing yourself into palatability. Take Sarah, a 29-year-old who described her social life as "a never-ending audition." With her partner, she laughed a little too loudly at jokes that didn't land. With friends, she swallowed her political opinions to avoid being "too much." At work, her voice softened, her ideas shrank, her posture folded—all to evade the label of "aggressive."

"It's like I'm a ghost," she confessed one evening, her voice trembling. "I'm there, but I'm not *allowed* to be there. The real me would ruin the scene."

Here's the brutal irony: The more Sarah contorted herself to fit in, the wider the chasm grew between her and others. Every suppressed thought, every stifled impulse, became a brick in a wall she couldn't see. Loneliness thrived in this divide—not because she was unseen, but because she was *unseen on purpose*. Her brain registered this dissonance as a threat, flooding her body with cortisol, the same stress hormone that primes us for fight-or-flight. *You are not safe here*, it whispered. *Not as you are.*

The Self You've Learned to Despise

Then there was Mark, 34, who spent hours rehearsing sentences before meetings, terrified his stammer would betray him. He avoided mirrors, hated photos of himself, and replayed social interactions like horror films: *Why did I laugh like that? Why did I stand like that?* His loneliness wasn't rooted in a lack of people—it was in the conviction that the person they'd encounter wasn't worthy of love.

This is loneliness's most sinister symptom: self-loathing so visceral, it metastasizes into isolation. Studies show that chronic loneliness alters brain structure, shrinking the prefrontal cortex—responsible for rational thought—and amplifying activity in the amygdala, the brain's fear center. Translation: The lonelier you feel, the more your brain becomes hypervigilant for rejection, interpreting neutral faces as disdain, pauses in conversation as judgment, and your own reflection as proof of inadequacy.

You become a prisoner of your perceived flaws, convinced your true self is a burden to others. So you preemptively exile yourself—ghosting friends, skipping parties, clinging to superficial interactions—to spare the world the inconvenience of *you*.

—

The Corrosive Cycle: How Loneliness Breeds Loneliness

Loneliness isn't passive; it's a self-reinforcing loop. The more you mask, the less authentic connection you experience. The less connection you feel, the more you fixate on your perceived unworthiness. Like a virus, it mutates, warping your behavior:

Hypervigilance: You scan rooms for signs of disinterest, interpreting crossed arms or yawns as personal rejections.
- Self-Sabotage: You bail on plans, convinced others will regret inviting you.
- Cynicism: You dismiss kindness as pity, compliments as lies, love as a transaction.

Neuroscientists call this “social withdrawal syndrome”—a state where the brain, starved of meaningful connection, rewires itself to prefer isolation. It’s not that you don’t *want* relationships; it’s that your nervous system now equates intimacy with danger.

But what if this agony isn't a life sentence—but a reckoning?

Loneliness forces you to confront the lies you've absorbed: "I am unlovable. I must earn belonging. My truth is a liability." It shoves you into the chasm between who you are and who you pretend to be, demanding a choice: Keep performing, or tear down the mask?

This is the paradox: Within loneliness's grip lies the seed of liberation. That voice whispering "You don't belong here" isn't your enemy—it's a distorted echo of a deeper truth: "You don't belong in this cage."

A Glimpse Beyond the Void

By the end of this book, you'll understand why "fighting" loneliness only tightens its grip—and how leaning into its discomfort can unravel a life you no longer recognize as yours. But first, we must dissect its anatomy.

In the next chapter, we'll delve into the biology of loneliness: How it alters your cells, hacks your immune system, and literally shortens your lifespan. You'll meet a woman whose chronic loneliness manifested as autoimmune disease, and a man whose recovery began not with friendship—but with a startling encounter with his own reflection.

The journey is harrowing. The reward? A self that needs no mask. Relationships that demand no performance. A life where belonging isn't something you earn—but something you embody.

The ghost in the room is you. It's time to step into the light.

Chapter 2

The Biology of Loneliness

How Isolation Rewires Your Body and Mind

Loneliness isn't just a feeling. It's a biological storm—a silent, invisible force that reshapes your cells, hacks your immune system, and chips away at your lifespan.

It's not just in your head. It's in your blood, your bones, your very DNA. This chapter isn't about emotions. It's about science. It's about understanding how loneliness—that ache you can't quite name—rewires your body and mind, turning you into a stranger to yourself.

Meet 42-year-old Clara, a woman who seemed to have it all: a successful career, a loving family, a life that looked perfect on paper. But beneath the surface, she was drowning. "I was always the strong one," she says. "The one who held everything together. But inside, I felt like I was falling apart." Clara's loneliness began subtly. She'd smile at parties but leave feeling emptier than when she arrived. She'd scroll through social media, envying the connections she couldn't seem to make. Over time, the loneliness became physical. She developed chronic fatigue, joint pain, and a rash that wouldn't go away.

Doctors were baffled. They ran tests, prescribed medications, but nothing worked. Finally, a rheumatologist asked a question no one else had: "How are you, really?" Clara broke down. "I told her everything," she says. "The isolation, the exhaustion, the feeling that no one really knew me. That's when she said, 'Your body is trying to tell you something.'" Clara was diagnosed with lupus, an autoimmune disease where the body attacks itself. "The doctor explained that chronic stress—including loneliness—can trigger autoimmune responses," she says. "My body was literally turning on itself because I felt so disconnected from the world."

For 35-year-old Daniel, loneliness wasn't just emotional. It was existential. "I felt like a ghost," he says. "I'd go to work, come home, and stare at the walls. I didn't know who I was anymore." Daniel's breaking point came one night when he caught his reflection in a store window. "I didn't recognize the person staring back at me," he says. "He looked tired, sad, empty. I thought, "Is this really me?"That moment sparked a journey of self-discovery. Daniel started therapy, began journaling, and even tried meditation—something he'd always dismissed as "woo-woo." Slowly, he began to reconnect with himself. "I realized that my loneliness wasn't just about other people," he says. "It was about me. I'd abandoned myself somewhere along the way."

Clara and Daniel's stories aren't just anecdotes. They're backed by science. Research shows that chronic loneliness triggers a cascade of biological changes. Loneliness increases inflammation, which damages cells and accelerates aging. It's like pouring acid on your DNA. It weakens your immune system, making you more susceptible to infections, diseases, and even cancer. It shrinks the prefrontal cortex (responsible for rational thought) and amplifies activity in the amygdala (the brain's fear center). Translation: The lonelier you feel, the harder it is to think clearly and the easier it is to spiral into fear and paranoia. Chronic loneliness increases mortality risk by 26%—equivalent to smoking 15 cigarettes a day. It's not just a mental health issue. It's a public health crisis.

Loneliness isn't just a lack of connection. It's a rupture of the self. It's the gap between who you are and who you think you should be. It's the voice that whispers, "You're not enough."But here's the truth: Loneliness isn't your enemy. It's a mirror—a merciless reflection of the fractures within. For Daniel, that mirror was literal. "Seeing myself in the window was the wake-up call I needed," he says. "It forced me to confront the void I'd been running from."

Chapter 3
The Imposter's Manifesto—When the World Becomes a Mirror You Can't Escape

You weren't born hating your laugh. You didn't come into this world rehearsing conversations in the shower or editing your personality like a disposable Instagram draft. But somewhere along the way, you became a collage of everyone else's expectations—a patchwork of *"Don't be too loud," "Smile more," "Act normal,"* and *"Who do you think you are?"* This chapter isn't about loneliness. It's about identity theft. Not the kind that drains your bank account, but the slow, spiritual robbery of your authenticity. The moment you traded your quirks for approval, your truth for tolerance, and your voice for a script written by strangers. Welcome to the imposter's paradox: The more you contort yourself to avoid judgment, the more you become a stranger worth judging.

Imagine carrying a mental Yelp review page everywhere you go. *3/5 stars—awkward eye contact.

1/5 stars—laughs at their own jokes. 4/5 stars—good listeners (but only because they never speak).* For 31-year-old Jamie, this isn't hypothetical. She celebrates her personality based on real and imagined critiques: *"My ex said I was clingy, so now I play aloof."* *"A coworker mocked my hobbies, so I call them 'guilty pleasures.'"* *"My mom said I'd look prettier, so I eat salads in public and binge in private."* The science of absorption reveals that the brain processes social rejection similarly to physical pain. But chronic fear of judgment goes further—it hijacks your self-concept. Neuroimaging shows that people who chronically people-please have reduced activity in the prefrontal cortex, the part of the brain responsible for self-awareness, and heightened activity in the amygdala, the brain's threat detector. In other words, you lose touch with who you are because your brain is too busy predicting how others will weaponize your authenticity. You don't just *hear* opinions. You *metabolize* them. They become the voice in your head, the critic in your mirror, the editor of your every word.

Loneliness makes you invisible, but fear of hatred makes you hyper-visible. You start seeing yourself through a warped lens of assumed disdain: *That barista sighed—was my order annoying?* *They didn't text back—do they regret knowing me?* *I shared a vulnerable story—do they think I'm pathetic?* For 27-year-old Dev, this paranoia became a prison. He deleted social media posts if they didn't get enough likes within an hour. He memorized coworkers' coffee orders to avoid being "difficult." He even wore neutral-colored clothes to avoid "standing out." *"It's like living in a haunted house,"* he says, *"where every crack is proof someone's laughing at me."* Research reveals that fearing social exclusion triggers the same primal panic as being hunted by predators. But humans have a cruel twist—we *imagine* the hunt. A 2023 study found that 68% of self-reported "unlikable" traits were purely speculative. Participants *assumed* others hated their quirks, only to discover those quirks were what made them memorable. Yet the imposter's mind clings to its narrative: *Better to be hated for a lie than risk being known.*

Here's the truth no one tells you: Faking your way through life isn't sustainable. It's a debt that compounds. Meet Elena, 38, who spent years being the "perfect" daughter, wife, and employee—until she collapsed mid-meeting, sobbing uncontrollably. *“I realized I hadn’t made a single choice for myself in a decade,”* she says. *“I was a puppet, but everyone else held the strings.”* The anatomy of a breakdown is brutal. First, there’s cognitive dissonance: Your soul knows you’re lying. The stress of maintaining a façade floods your body with cortisol, eroding your immune system and focus. Then comes emotional numbness: Joy requires authenticity. When you fake connections, even “happy” moments feel hollow. Finally, there’s identity erosion: Over time, you forget who you were before the performance. The imposter isn’t a role—it’s your default. You stop trusting your instincts, desires, and boundaries. You date people you dislike to avoid being “picky.” You stay in jobs that drain you to seem “grateful.” You laugh when you want to scream, stay silent when you want to roar, and shrink when you want to take up space.

The cruelest consequence? The imposter becomes your only witness. You scroll through photos of yourself at parties, vacations, weddings—and can’t recognize the person smiling back. *Who is that?* you wonder. *What do they want? What do they fear?* You’ve become a ghost in your own life, haunting the shell of someone you think the world might tolerate.

But there's a rebellion stirring—one this book will guide you to unleash. The imposter's reign thrives on one lie: *You are what others say you are.* But buried beneath the borrowed identities and phantom judgments, your raw, unedited self remains. The road back to yourself is paved with terrifying truths. But the alternative—a life of borrowed opinions and phantom joy—is no life at all. The imposter's manifesto ends here. Your story begins now.

Chapter 4
The Rebellion of the Real
Unearthing Your Buried Desires

There comes a moment in life when the masks you've worn for so long begin to crack. The persona you've built to please others, to fit in, to survive, starts to feel less like armor and more like a cage. You look in the mirror and see a stranger staring back at someone you don't recognize, someone you don't even like. And in that moment, a quiet rebellion begins. This chapter is about that rebellion. It's about exhuming the desires you buried long ago, confronting the critics both inside your head and out and rewriting the manifesto of your life. It's about the man who quit his law career to become a stand-up comedian at 45, the woman who rebuilt her life after admitting her marriage was a performance, and the teenager who traded viral validation for vulnerability and found belonging.

For most of his life, Mark was the picture of success. He had a thriving law career, a beautiful home, and a family who loved him. But beneath the surface, he was drowning. "I felt like a fraud," he says. "Every day, I'd put on a suit, go to court, and argue cases I didn't care about. I was living someone else's life." Mark's breaking point came during a particularly grueling trial. "I was standing in front of the judge, and I just froze," he recalls. "I couldn't remember my argument. I couldn't even remember why I was there. All I could think was, "What am I doing with my life?"That night, Mark did something he hadn't done in years: He went to a comedy club. "I'd always loved making people laugh," he says. "But I'd buried that part of myself because it didn't fit the 'serious lawyer' image." As he watched the comedians on stage, something inside him shifted. “I realized I’d rather bomb on stage than succeed in a courtroom.” At 45, Mark quit his law career and became a stand-up comedian. “It wasn’t easy,” he admits. “I lost clients, friends, even some family members who thought I was throwing my life away. But for the first time, I felt alive. I was finally being *me.*”

Sarah had spent 20 years playing the role of the perfect wife. She kept the house spotless, cooked gourmet meals, and supported her husband’s career without complaint. But behind closed doors, she was miserable. “I felt like a character in a play,” she says. “I was performing, not living.” The turning point came during a family vacation. “We were at the beach, and my husband was on his phone the whole time,” Sarah recalls. “I looked at him and thought, ‘Is this it? Is this all my life is going to be?” That night, Sarah made a decision: She was done performing. “I told my husband how I felt,” she says. “I told him I wasn’t happy, that I felt invisible. It was the hardest conversation of my life.” The marriage ended, but Sarah’s journey was just beginning. She went back to school, started a new career, and rediscovered passions she’d long forgotten.

“I learned to paint, to dance, to laugh again,” she says. “I realized I didn’t need to be perfect to be loved. I just needed to be “me.”

For 16-year-old Mia, social media was everything. She spent hours curating her feed, taking the perfect selfies, and chasing likes. “I thought if I could just get enough followers, I’d feel like I belonged,” she says. But the more validation she got, the emptier she felt. “I’d post a photo and wait for the likes to roll in,” she says. “But as soon as they did, I’d feel this crushing disappointment. It was never enough.” Mia’s turning point came during a school retreat. “We were sitting around a campfire, and someone started telling a story,” she recalls. “It was raw, real, and vulnerable. And for the first time, I felt a connection that social media had never given me.” That night, Mia made a decision: She was done chasing likes. She deleted her social media accounts and started sharing her real self with the people around her. “It was scary at first,” she admits. “But the more I opened up, the more I realized I wasn’t alone. People didn’t want perfection. They wanted “real.”

Mark, Sarah, and Mia’s stories show that rebellion isn’t about destroying your life. It’s about reclaiming it. It’s about digging up the desires you buried, silencing the critics—both inside your head and out—and rewriting the manifesto of your life. Here's how you can start: Exhume your desires. What did you love before the world told you what to love? What makes you feel alive? What would you do if no one was watching? Confront the critics. The voices in your head aren't the truth. They're echoes of old fears and expectations. Challenge them. Replace them with your own voice. Rewrite your manifesto. What do you stand for? What do you want your life to be about? Write it down. Make it bold. Make it yours. Embrace vulnerability. Real connection comes from being real. Share your struggles, your dreams, your messy, imperfect self. You'll find that people love you more for it, not less.

The rebellion of the real isn't easy. It requires courage, vulnerability, and a willingness to let go of the life you've built to please others. But it's worth it. Because on the other side of rebellion is freedom. On the other side of fear is joy. On the other side of the mask is *you.* Turn the page. Start your rebellion. The world needs the real you—not the performance, not the persona, not the perfect image. Just you.

Reflection Question: Think of one desire you've buried. What's one small step you can take today to exhume it? The rebellion begins with you.

Chapter 5
The Monster in the Mirror
How Society Feeds on Your Hunger to Belong

The Day the Mirror Spoke Back
You know the ritual. You wake up, shuffle to the bathroom, and brace yourself. The mirror doesn't just reflect your face—it hisses. *Too wide hips. Thinning hair. Crooked teeth. Weak chin.* You tally flaws like sins, each one a shackle to the beast pacing inside you: **Loneliness**. But this isn't just emptiness. This is a ravenous, snarling thing, fed daily by the world's whispered lies: *You are not enough. You will never be enough.*

Loneliness isn't passive. It's a predator. And modern society? It's the hunter that raised it, sharpening its claws on beauty standards, social hierarchies, and algorithmic rage. This chapter isn't a warning. It's a autopsy of how we became prey.

The Monster's Diet: Why You'll Never Be Full
Loneliness thrives on lack—but society manufactures that lack. Instagram isn't just an app. It's a dopamine slot machine where you gamble your self-worth for likes, betting against airbrushed influencers and their "perfect" lives. Every scroll is a crumb tossed to the monster: *Why don't you look like her? Why isn't your life this vibrant?*

Meet Lila, 22, who starved herself into the hospital trying to mimic TikTok beauty filters. "I'd look in the mirror and see a monster," she says. "But the real monster was the voice saying, *'You're not pretty enough to be loved.'*"

The science of scarcity: Studies show that exposure to idealized images triggers the brain's anterior cingulate cortex—the same region that lights up during physical pain. Beauty standards aren't trends. They're trauma. And loneliness? It's the infection that festers in the wound.

The Chains You Can't See: Social Class and the Myth of "Enough"

You've felt it—the quiet shame of "not measuring up." The college dropout at family reunions, dodging questions about their job. The single friend at weddings, faking smiles through toasts about "soulmates." The immigrant parent working triple shifts, whispering, "We're still not there yet."

Loneliness isn't just emotional. It's systemic. Social media sells the lie that anyone can "hustle" their way to wealth, love, and status—ignoring the chains of poverty, racism, and generational trauma. For 40-year-old Marcus, a Black man raised in a food desert, loneliness tastes like survivor's guilt. "I got the corporate job, the suburban house,"he says. "But I'm too 'white' for my old neighborhood and too 'other' for my new one. I don't belong anywhere."

The hierarchy of belonging: Research reveals that perceived social rank directly impacts mental health. The lower you believe you are on the ladder, the louder the monster growls. You internalize the hierarchy, punishing yourself for “failing” to climb it. But the ladder is rigged—and the monster *designed* it.

The Poisoned Well: How Media Sells You Solutions to a Problem It Created

Every ad, every show, every post is a mirror held up to your deepest insecurities:

- “Lose 20 lbs and finally be confident!” (Translation: Your body is a problem to solve.)
- “This $200 serum will fix your aging skin!” (Translation: Your face is expiring.)
- “Go viral or die irrelevant!” (Translation: Your existence requires an audience.)

Loneliness isn’t a flaw. It’s a commodity. Corporations weaponize your hunger for connection to sell you crap you don’t need, dangling “belonging” like a carrot on a stick. For 19-year-old Ryan, that carrot was a luxury watch he couldn't afford. "I bought it to impress guys I hated," he admits. "I wore it to parties where no one looked me in the eye. It felt like wearing a coffin."

The cycle of consumption: Buy to fit in → realize you still feel empty → buy more. The monster grows fat on your desperation, while society profits from your bleeding need to belong.

The Final Trap: Self-Mockery as Survival

You've done it—laughed off your dreams as "silly," called yourself "ugly" before others could, played the clown to avoid being the target. Self-deprecation feels like armor, but it's a Trojan horse. For 36-year-old Priya, sarcasm became her prison. "I'd joke about my stretch marks, my dead-end job, my bad dates," she says. "People laughed, so I thought I was winning. But every joke was a brick in the wall between me and real connection."

Self-mockery is loneliness's sharpest trick. It lets the monster mimic your voice, so you'll cage yourself. You think you’re beating others to the punch. Really, you’re just punching yourself.

The Bleeding Edge: When the Monster Wins

Here’s the truth they’ll never post on Instagram: Loneliness kills. Not metaphorically. Literally. Chronic loneliness increases mortality risk by 26%—equivalent to smoking 15 cigarettes a day. It inflames your arteries, weakens your immune system, and corrodes your mind. But society won’t tell you that. Why?

Because dead people don’t buy serums. Broken people don’t question the system. And the monster? It’s too busy feeding.

A Spark in the Dark

But this isn’t the end. It’s a crossroads.

The monster wants you to believe you’re powerless—that society’s chains are unbreakable, that your hunger will never be satisfied. But what if the key to your cage has been in your hand all along?

In the next chapter, we'll ignite The Rebellion of the Unseen: how to starve the monster by rejecting its lies, reclaim your voice from the jaws of media, and forge belonging on your own terms. You'll meet a former model who set her beauty standards on fire, a billionaire's son who abandoned wealth to find purpose in a homeless shelter, and a community of "misfits" who rewrote the rules of connection—and discovered the monster hates the light.

The world wants you silent, small, and hungry. But you? You're a wildfire waiting to burn.

Turn the page. Break the chain. The monster's reign ends when you stop feeding it—and start feeding you.

Chapter 6

The Snake in the Garden

How Loneliness Poisons the Love You Already Have

Picture this: You're sitting at a family dinner, surrounded by laughter, warmth, and the people who've loved you since before you took your first breath. Your parents ask about your job. Your sibling teases you about your childhood quirks. Your partner squeezes your hand under the table. It's perfect. But inside, a storm rages. They don't get it, you think. They don't see how hard I'm working. They don't understand my dreams. You force a smile, but the resentment builds. Later, you snap at your mom for "nagging," ignore your partner's texts, and cancel plans with your best friend. "They don't appreciate me," you tell yourself.

But here's the truth: The problem isn't them. It's the snake in your mind—loneliness—whispering lies about your worth and twisting love into neglect. This chapter isn't about losing people. It's about pushing them away while blaming them for the distance.

Loneliness isn't always about being alone. Sometimes, it's about feeling unseen—even by the people who see you best. For 30-year-old Sam, this illusion became a prison. "I worked 80-hour weeks to impress my dad,"* he says. "When I got promoted, I called him, expecting a parade. He just said, 'I'm proud of you, but don't forget to take care of yourself.' I was furious. I thought,

'Why doesn't he care?' But the truth? He cared too much. He didn't want the promotion. He wanted me.

The harder you work to prove your worth, the emptier you feel. You chase goals, thinking they'll fill the void, but the void isn't in your achievements. It's in your inability to see yourself as worthy—just as you are. Loneliness doesn't just distort your self-worth. It distorts your relationships. You start to blame: "They don't appreciate me."* You start to feel ashamed: "I'm not good enough for them."
You start to isolate: "I'll just handle this alone."

For 27-year-old Priya, this cycle cost her a decade-long friendship. "I was so focused on building my career, I stopped showing up for my best friend," she says. "When she got engaged, I was too busy to help plan the wedding. She stopped calling, and I told myself, 'See? She never cared.' But the truth? I pushed her away. I was so scared of being unimportant, I made myself invisible."

Studies show that chronic loneliness increases sensitivity to social slights. You interpret neutral actions as rejection, kindness as pity, and love as obligation.

The more you withdraw, the more your loved ones pull away—not because they don't care, but because they don't know how to reach you.

Here's the hardest truth: Loneliness doesn't just hurt you. It hurts the people who love you. For 45-year-old Maria, this realization came too late. "I was so obsessed with being the 'perfect' mom, I stopped being present," she says. "I'd yell at my kids for interrupting my work, then cry myself to sleep because they stopped coming to me for hugs. One day, my daughter said, 'I miss you, Mom.' I realized I'd been so focused on providing for them, I forgot to be there for them."

Every ignored call, every snapped response, every missed moment chips away at the bonds you cherish. Over time, the people who once knew you best become strangers—not because they stopped loving you, but because you stopped letting them in.

Loneliness is a master manipulator. It convinces you that your worth is tied to your achievements, that your loved ones don't understand you, and that you're better off alone. But these are lies. The truth? The people who love you don't care about your job title, your bank account, or your Instagram followers. They care about you—your laugh, your quirks, your presence.

For 33-year-old Jake, this truth was a lifeline. "I spent years trying to impress my wife with fancy gifts and big gestures," he says. "Then one day, she said, 'I don't need diamonds. I just need you.' That's when I realized: Loneliness wasn't about being alone. It was about forgetting how to be loved."

But this isn't the end. It's a wake-up call. Loneliness thrives in the gaps between us—but those gaps can be bridged. The first step is recognizing the snake's lies and choosing to see the love that's always been there.

—----------

Chapter 7

The Silent Epidemic

How Loneliness Kills While the World Looks Away

You've heard the stories. The coworker who always smiled but never spoke about her weekends. The neighbor who waved every morning but whose blinds stayed drawn. The classmate who cracked jokes but sat alone at lunch. Then, one day, they're gone. The news whispers the word no one wants to say: suicide. And the world moves on.

Loneliness isn't just a feeling. It's a disease—a slow, insidious poison that eats away at your will to live. But here's the cruelest part: Society has normalized it. We've turned loneliness into a punchline ("Forever alone!"), a hashtag (#lonelybutstrong), a rite of passage ("Everyone feels this way!"). But when the laughter fades, the silence remains. And in that silence, the monster feasts. This chapter isn't just about loneliness. It's about the lives it steals while we pretend it's harmless.

Loneliness doesn't kill you overnight. It's a slow bleed, a thousand tiny cuts. It's the unanswered text you stare at for hours, wondering why no one has replied. It's the party invitation you decline because you're "busy," even though you're just sitting at home, scrolling through social media, watching everyone else live their lives. It's the mirror that reflects not your face, but your failures—the weight you haven't lost, the wrinkles you can't hide, the person you think you're supposed to be but can't quite become.

For 28-year-old Alex, the cuts became too many to count. "I'd sit in my car after work, crying because I had nowhere to go," he says. "I'd scroll through my phone, but no one checked on me. I started to think, 'If I disappeared, would anyone notice?" Loneliness triggers a cascade of biological changes. Cortisol levels spike, inflaming your body and brain. Serotonin and dopamine—the "feel-good" chemicals—plummet, leaving you numb. Over time, chronic loneliness rewires your brain to see pain as inevitable and connection as impossible. It's not just in your head. It's in your cells.

Society doesn't just ignore loneliness—it normalizes it. We romanticize the "strong, silent type" who suffers in silence. We glorify busyness, equating isolation with productivity. We dismiss cries for help as "attention-seeking" or "dramatic." For 24-year-old Mia, this normalization was a death sentence. "I told my friends I felt lonely, and they laughed," she recalls. "They said, *'Join the club!'* But I wasn't looking for a club. I was looking for a lifeline." The statistics scream: Suicide rates have skyrocketed, with loneliness cited as a leading factor. Yet, we treat it like a personal failing, not a public health crisis. We tell people to "cheer up" or "get out more," as if loneliness is a choice, not a disease. But here's the truth: Loneliness isn't a weakness. It's a wound. And untreated wounds fester.

Loneliness doesn't just make you sad. It makes you hopeless. It convinces you that you are unlovable, that your pain is invisible, that your absence wouldn't matter. For 35-year-old Daniel, the spiral began with a breakup. "I felt like a ghost," he says. "I'd walk through crowds, but no one saw me. I'd talk, but no one listened. I started to think, 'If I'm already invisible, what's the point of existing?" Research shows that chronic loneliness increases suicide risk by 50%. It's not just the emotional pain—it's the certainty that the pain will never end. Loneliness doesn't just steal your joy. It steals your future.

Loneliness doesn't discriminate. It preys on the elderly widow, the bullied teen, the overworked parent, the immigrant far from home. It thrives in the gaps we refuse to see: the coworker who eats lunch alone, the neighbor who never has visitors, the friend who stopped posting on social media. For 42-year-old Sarah, a teacher, the warning signs were there. "I had a student who always sat by himself," she says. "I thought,'He's just shy.' Then he tried to take his own life. I'll never forgive myself for not seeing the pain behind his silence." The cost of indifference is staggering. Every suicide is a ripple, tearing through families, friendships, and communities. Yet, we keep pretending loneliness is "normal."

But this isn't the end. It's a call to arms. Loneliness is a disease, but it's not incurable. The first step is breaking the silence—refusing to normalize the pain, refusing to look away.

The monster thrives in silence. But together, we can drown it out. Turn the page. Break the silence. The world needs your voice.

Trigger Warning: If you or someone you know is struggling with loneliness or suicidal thoughts, please reach out to a trusted friend, family member, or mental health professional. You are not alone, and your life matters.

——————

Chapter 8

The Revolution of Connection
How to Break the Silence and Rebuild Bridges

Loneliness is a silent epidemic, but it doesn't have to be a life sentence. It's a disease, yes, but one that can be cured—not with medicine, but with connection. The first step is breaking the silence. Refusing to normalize the pain. Refusing to look away. This chapter is about starting a revolution—a revolution of connection. It's about spotting the signs of loneliness in yourself and others, rebuilding the bridges burned by despair, and creating a world where no one has to suffer in silence.

You'll meet a man who turned his grief into a global support network, a teen who saved a classmate's life with a single question, and a community that replaced stigma with solidarity. Their stories are proof that loneliness doesn't have to win.

The Man Who Turned Grief into Connection

When Mark lost his wife to cancer, he didn't just lose his partner. He lost his anchor. "I felt like I was drowning," he says. "I didn't know how to be alone. I didn't know how to ask for help."

For months, Mark isolated himself. He stopped answering calls. He stopped going to work. He even stopped leaving the house. "I thought I was protecting myself," he says. "But really, I was just sinking deeper into the void."

One day, Mark stumbled across an online forum for people who had lost loved ones. "I didn't plan to post anything," he says. "But then I saw this message from a woman who had lost her husband. She described exactly how I felt—the emptiness, the guilt, the fear. For the first time in months, I didn't feel alone."

Mark started sharing his own story. He wrote about the good days and the bad days. He wrote about the memories that made him laugh and the ones that made him cry. And slowly, something incredible happened: People started responding.

"I realized that my pain could help others," Mark says. "It didn't take away my grief, but it gave it meaning."

Today, Mark runs a global support network for people dealing with loss. “Loneliness thrives in silence,” he says. “But so does connection. All it takes is one person to say, ‘I see you. I hear you. You’re not alone.’”

The Teen Who Asked One Question

For 16-year-old Emma, high school was a minefield. “Everyone was so focused on themselves,” she says. “No one really *saw* each other.”

One day, Emma noticed that her classmate, Jake, seemed off. “He was usually so outgoing, but that day, he was quiet. He looked sad.”

Emma didn’t know Jake well. They’d never even had a real conversation. But something inside her told her to reach out.

“I walked up to him and said, ‘Are you okay?’” Emma recalls. “He looked at me like no one had ever asked him that before. Then he started crying.”

Jake opened up to Emma about his struggles with depression and his thoughts of suicide. “I didn’t know what to say,” Emma admits. “But I listened. And I think that’s what he needed most.”

Emma encouraged Jake to talk to a counselor, and she stayed by his side as he started his journey toward healing. “That one question changed everything,” Jake says. “It made me feel like I mattered.”

Emma’s story is a reminder that connection doesn’t have to be complicated. Sometimes, it’s as simple as asking, “Are you okay?”

The Community That Replaced Stigma with Solidarity
In a small town in Ohio, loneliness was a way of life. “People kept to themselves,” says 45-year-old Sarah, a lifelong resident. “We’d smile and wave, but no one really talked.”

Everything changed when a local teenager died by suicide. “It shook the whole town,” Sarah says. “We realized we'd been so focused on our own lives, we hadn't noticed the pain right in front of us."

Determined to make a change, Sarah and a group of neighbors started a community initiative called "Together Tuesdays." Every week, they'd gather in the town square to share stories, play games, and just be together.

"At first, people were hesitant," Sarah says. "But slowly, they started opening up. They talked about their struggles with loneliness, their fears, their hopes. It was like a dam had broken."

Today, "Together Tuesdays" is a cornerstone of the community. "We've replaced stigma with solidarity," Sarah says. "We've shown that it's okay to not be okay—and that we're stronger together."

The Revolution: How to Start Connecting

Mark, Emma, and Sarah's stories show that connection is possible—but it requires courage, compassion, and a willingness to break the silence. Here's how you can start:

1. Spot the Signs: Loneliness isn't always obvious. It can look like withdrawal, irritability, or even overworking. Pay attention to the people around you. If someone seems off, reach out.

2. Ask the Question: "Are you okay?" These three words can save a life. Don't wait for someone to ask for help. Be the one to start the conversation.

3. Share Your Story: Vulnerability is contagious. When you open up about your struggles, you give others permission to do the same.

4. Create Spaces for Connection: Whether it's a weekly gathering or a simple text chain, create opportunities for people to come together.

5. Replace Stigma with Solidarity: Loneliness thrives in shame. Break the cycle by normalizing conversations about mental health and connection.

A Glimmer in the Darkness

Loneliness is a silent epidemic, but it doesn't have to be a life sentence. The revolution of connection starts with you. It starts with a question, a story, a moment of vulnerability.

The silence ends here. The connection begins now.

Chapter 9

The Healing

Rebuilding Your Sense of Self and Reconnecting with Others

Loneliness isn't just an emotion. It's a wound—one that festers when left untreated. But wounds, no matter how deep, can heal. This chapter is about that healing. It's about rebuilding your sense of self, reconnecting with the people you've pushed away, and creating a life where loneliness no longer has a place. It's about the woman who repaired her relationship with her estranged father, the man who learned to parent his inner child, and the community that turned pain into purpose.

The Woman Who Found Her Father

For 34-year-old Maria, loneliness had always felt like a family heirloom—something passed down through generations. Her father had left when she was six, and the void he left behind shaped her life in ways she didn't fully understand. "I spent years trying to fill that emptiness," she says. "I dated men who were emotionally unavailable, just like him. I pushed people away before they could leave me. I even avoided having kids because I was scared I'd fail them, like he failed me."

But one day, something shifted. Maria was cleaning out her childhood home when she found an old photo of her father. "He was holding me on his shoulders, and we were both laughing," she says. "I realized I didn't just miss him. I missed the possibility of him—the father he could have been."

That photo sparked a journey Maria never expected. She reached out to her father, not knowing if he'd respond. To her surprise, he did. "The first conversation was awkward," she admits. "We didn't know how to talk to each other. But over time, we found our way. He apologized for leaving. I apologized for shutting him out. We started building something new—not the relationship we should have had, but the one we could have now."

Maria's story isn't about forgiveness or reconciliation. It's about healing. "I didn't get my father back," she says. "But I got myself back. I stopped carrying the weight of his absence and started living for my own presence."

The Man Who Parented His Inner Child

For 28-year-old Jake, loneliness wasn't just a feeling. It was a voice—a constant whisper telling him he wasn't good enough. "I was always trying to prove myself," he says. "At work, in relationships, even with friends. I thought if I could just be perfect, I'd finally feel like I belonged."

But perfection is a moving target, and Jake was exhausted. "I hit a breaking point," he says. "I was sitting in my apartment, staring at the wall, and I just started crying. I felt like that little kid who was always picked last in gym class, who never felt like he was enough."

That moment was the start of Jake's healing journey. He began therapy, where he learned about the concept of "reparenting"—the idea of nurturing your inner child, the part of you that still carries the wounds of the past. "I started talking to that little kid inside me," Jake says. "I'd tell him, 'You're enough. You're loved. You don't have to prove anything.' It felt silly at first, but it changed everything."

Jake's healing wasn't linear. There were setbacks, moments of doubt, and days when the loneliness felt overwhelming. But over time, he began to feel whole. "I realized I didn't need to be perfect to be loved," he says. "I just needed to be me."

The Community That Turned Pain into Purpose

Loneliness thrives in isolation, but it withers in connection. For the residents of a small town in Ohio, this truth became the foundation of their healing.

It started with a single post on a community Facebook page. “I’m lonely,” wrote 42-year-old Sarah, a single mother of two. “I don’t know if anyone else feels this way, but I just needed to say it.”

To Sarah’s surprise, the post went viral—not on the internet, but in her town. Dozens of people responded, sharing their own stories of loneliness. “It was like this floodgate opened,” Sarah says. “People were saying things they’d never said out loud before. It was heartbreaking, but it was also beautiful.”

That post sparked a movement. The town started hosting weekly gatherings—potlucks, game nights, even a book club. “We called it the ‘No More Loneliness’ project,” Sarah says. “It wasn’t about fixing anyone. It was about showing up, being real, and reminding each other that we’re not alone.”

The project transformed the town. People who had been strangers became friends. Families who had been isolated found support. And Sarah? She found her purpose. “I used to think loneliness was my burden to carry,” she says. “Now I see it as my calling. I want to help people connect, not just in my town, but everywhere.”

The Healing: How to Start

Maria, Jake, and Sarah’s stories show that healing is possible—but it requires courage, vulnerability, and a willingness to take the first step. Here’s how you can start:

1. Reconnect with Your Past: Healing begins with understanding. Reflect on the experiences that shaped your loneliness. What wounds are you carrying? How have they influenced your life?

2. Nurture Your Inner Child: That little kid inside you still needs love. Talk to them. Comfort them. Give them the acceptance and validation they never received.

3. Reach Out: Loneliness thrives in silence. Share your story with someone you trust. You might be surprised by how many people feel the same way.

4. Build Community: Connection is the antidote to loneliness. Join a group, start a project, or simply show up for the people around you.

5. Be Patient: Healing isn't a destination. It's a journey. There will be setbacks, but every step forward is a victory.

A Glimmer in the Darkness

Loneliness is a wound, but it's also a teacher. It shows you where you've abandoned yourself, where you've disconnected from others, and where you've bought into society's lies.

Healing isn't easy. It's a journey—one that requires courage, vulnerability, and patience. But it's also a journey worth taking. Because on the other side of loneliness is connection. On the other side of pain is joy. On the other side of the mask is *you*.

Turn the page. Start healing. The world needs the real you—not the mask, not the performance, not the fantasy. Just you.

Chapter 10

The Masks We Wear

How Society Turned us into Strangers to Ourselves

You know the drill. You wake up, scroll through Instagram, and see it—the highlight reel of humanity. Perfect smiles. Perfect bodies. Perfect lives. You sigh, grab your "confidence" playlist, and start the daily transformation: the makeup, the outfit, the practiced laugh, the scripted small talk. By the time you leave the house, you're ready. But ready for what? To impress strangers? To fit in? To survive? Here's the truth: You're not surviving. You're disappearing.

This chapter isn't about fitting in. It's about the cost of becoming a stranger to yourself—and the toxic society that profits from your vanishing act.

You weren't born with a mask. You learned to wear one. Maybe it started in school, when the "weird" kids were bullied. Maybe it was at work, when your boss praised your colleague for being "agreeable." Maybe it was on social media, where every post felt like a performance. For 29-year-old Nina, the mask became her armor. "I'd laugh at jokes I didn't find funny, agree with opinions I didn't share, and pretend to like people I couldn't stand," she says. "I thought I was being 'nice.' But really, I was erasing myself."

The science of people-pleasing reveals that suppressing your true self triggers the brain's stress response, releasing cortisol and adrenaline. Over time, this chronic stress rewires your brain to see authenticity as a threat and conformity as safety. The mask isn't just a facade. It's a cage.

Modern friendships aren't about connection. They're about curation. You don't bond over shared values or vulnerabilities. You bond over shared vibes—carefully crafted personas that mirror each other's masks. For 25-year-old Amir, this paradox cost him his closest friend. "We'd known each other since kindergarten," he says. "But as we got older, our friendship became a performance. We'd go out, take selfies, and post captions like 'Squad goals!' But we never talked about the hard stuff—our fears, our failures, our dreams. One day, I realized I didn't even know him anymore. And he didn't know me."

When friendships are built on masks, they crumble under pressure. You can't trust someone who only knows your facade—and you can't trust yourself to be real.

Here's the cruelest twist: The more masks you wear, the harder it becomes to spot the toxic people. You start to confuse manipulation for kindness, drama for passion, and exploitation for loyalty. For 32-year-old Sofia, this trap nearly destroyed her. "I had a friend who always 'supported' me," she says. "But her support came with strings. She'd guilt-trip me for spending time with other people, trash-talk anyone who disagreed with her, and make me feel like I owed her my loyalty. I thought she was my ride-or-die. Turns out, she was just toxic."

When you're wearing a mask, everyone else's mask looks real. Friends who only reach out when they need something, people who gossip about others but act sweet to your face, relationships that drain you more than they fill you—these are the red flags you miss.

The longer you wear the mask, the harder it is to take it off. You start to distrust your true self, believing it's unlikable, unworthy, or unlovable. For 36-year-old Carlos, this loss was devastating. "I spent so long trying to fit in, I forgot who I was," he says. "I'd look in the mirror and see a stranger. I didn't know what I liked, what I wanted, or even what I felt. I was just a collection of masks, trying to please everyone but myself."

The anatomy of self-erasure is a slow, painful process. First, you silence your thoughts, desires, and boundaries to avoid conflict. Then, you start to see your true self as a liability, not an asset. Finally, you lose touch with your instincts, intuition, and identity. You become a ghost in your own life, haunting the shell of someone you think the world might tolerate.

Do you know who you are now that you've read this? Strip away the makeup, the filters, the scripts, and the masks. Who's left? What do they want? What do they fear? What do they dream? If you don't know the answers, you're not alone. But you're also not doomed.

The masks we wear aren't just a personal choice. They're a societal sickness—one that thrives on our fear of rejection and our hunger for approval. But here's the truth: The world doesn't need more masks. It needs more you.

The masks may feel safe, but they're not alive. The real you? That's where the magic happens.

Chapter 11

The Unmasking How to Reclaim Your True Self and Build Authentic Connections

The mask has been your shield, your armor, your survival tool. But it's also been your prison. Every laugh you faked, every opinion you swallowed, every part of yourself you tucked away to fit in—it all added another layer to the mask, another brick to the wall between you and the world.

But here's the truth: The mask isn't protecting you anymore. It's suffocating you.

This chapter is about liberation. It's about peeling off the layers of performance, reconnecting with your true self, and building relationships that celebrate—not suffocate—your authenticity. It's about the former influencer who quit social media to find herself, the CEO who replaced "professionalism" with vulnerability, and the community that learned to love without masks.

The Influencer Who Quit the Highlight Reel

For 26-year-old Mia, life was a never-ending performance. As a social media influencer with over a million followers, she had perfected the art of the mask. Her feed was a curated masterpiece of flawless selfies, exotic vacations, and #blessed captions. But behind the filters, Mia was drowning.

"I was so focused on maintaining this perfect image that I forgot who I really was," she says. "I'd spend hours editing photos, crafting captions, and responding to comments. But at the end of the day, I felt empty. I had all these followers, but I didn't have any real connections."

Mia's breaking point came during a sponsored trip to Bali. "I was supposed to be living the dream," she says. "But I was miserable. I was surrounded by people, but I felt completely alone. I realized I wasn't living my life—I was performing it."

That day, Mia made a radical decision: She quit social media. "I deleted all my accounts and disappeared," she says. "At first, I was terrified. Social media was my identity. Without it, who was I?"

But as the weeks turned into months, Mia began to rediscover herself. She started painting again, something she hadn't done since high school. She reconnected with old friends, not through screens, but face-to-face. She even started a blog—not for likes or followers, but to share her journey of self-discovery.

"Quitting social media was the best thing I ever did," she says. "I realized that my worth isn't in how many people like me. It's in how much I like myself."

The CEO Who Embraced Vulnerability

For 42-year-old James, success had always been about control. As the CEO of a thriving tech company, he prided himself on his professionalism, his decisiveness, his ability to keep his emotions in check. But beneath the polished exterior, James was struggling.

"I thought being a leader meant being invincible," he says. "I never showed weakness, never asked for help, never admitted when I was wrong. But it was exhausting. I felt like I was carrying the weight of the world on my shoulders, and I had no one to share it with."

Everything changed during a company retreat. "We were doing this team-building exercise where we had to share something personal," James recalls. "I was planning to give my usual polished spiel, but something inside me snapped. I started talking about how lonely I felt, how much pressure I was under, how scared I was of failing. I thought everyone would lose respect for me. But the opposite happened."

James's vulnerability transformed the company culture. Employees started opening up about their own struggles. Collaboration improved. Trust deepened. Even the bottom line benefited. "I realized that being a leader isn't about being perfect," James says. "It's about being human."

The Community That Learned to Love Without Masks

In a small town in Oregon, a group of neighbors decided to do something radical: They created a "vulnerability circle." Every week, they would gather in someone's living room, share their struggles, and support each other without judgment.

For 34-year-old Sarah, the circle was a lifeline. "I'd always been the 'strong one' in my family," she says. "I never let anyone see me cry, never asked for help, never admitted when I was struggling. But in the circle, I didn't have to pretend. I could just be me."

The circle became a safe space for everyone involved. A single dad struggling to balance work and parenting. A retiree grappling with loneliness. A teenager navigating the pressures of social media. "We realized that we all had masks," Sarah says. "And we all wanted to take them off."

The Unmasking: How to Reclaim Your True Self

Mia, James, and Sarah's stories show that unmasking is possible—but it requires courage, vulnerability, and a willingness to let go of old ways of thinking. Here's how you can start:

1. Acknowledge the Mask: The first step to unmasking is recognizing that you're wearing one. What parts of yourself have you hidden to fit in? What roles have you been playing to please others?

2. Embrace Vulnerability: Vulnerability isn't weakness. It's strength. It's the courage to show up as you are, not as you think you should be. Start small: Share something real with someone you trust.

3. Rediscover Your Passions: What did you love before the world told you who to be? Reconnect with those passions, not for likes or approval, but for joy.

4. Build Authentic Connections: Surround yourself with people who celebrate your authenticity, not your mask.

Seek out relationships that are based on trust, not performance.

5. Practice Self-Compassion: Be kind to yourself as you unmask. It's not easy to let go of old habits, but every step toward authenticity is a step toward freedom.

A Glimmer in the Darkness

The mask may feel safe, but it's not alive. The real you? That's where the magic happens.

Think of one mask you wear regularly. What's one small step you can take today to let it go? The unmasking begins with you.

Chapter 12

The Roots of Loneliness

How the Seed Was Planted Before You Could Speak

The Day You Cried for the First Time

It starts earlier than you think. You're lying in a crib, swaddled in blankets, staring at a ceiling you don't understand. Your tiny body screams for warmth, for milk, for touch—for the one person who makes the world feel safe. But she's not there. Not yet.

So you cry. Not because you're spoiled. Not because you're dramatic. But because your survival depends on it.

This is where loneliness begins: in the gap between your need and its fulfillment. Before you know words, before you know faces, before you even know *you*, you know this ache.

This chapter isn't about blame. It's about tracing the roots of loneliness back to their origin—and understanding how they shaped the person you've become.

The Crib and the Void: When Loneliness Learns Your Name

As a baby, your world is small but vast. You don't understand time, so minutes feel like hours. You don't understand space, so a room feels like a universe. And when you're left alone in that universe, the void whispers: You are not enough to make them stay.

For 30-year-old Leila, this void never left. “My mom was a single parent,” she says. “She worked two jobs to keep us afloat, but I didn’t understand that as a kid. All I knew was that she wasn’t there when I cried. I grew up feeling like I had to earn love—that if I wasn’t ‘good,’ I’d be left alone again.”

The science of attachment: Studies show that early experiences of neglect or inconsistency shape the brain’s attachment system. If your needs aren't met consistently, you may grow up fearing abandonment—even in healthy relationships.

The crib is where loneliness learns your name. But it doesn’t stop there.

The Playground Paradox: When Belonging Costs You Yourself

Fast forward a few years. You’re on a playground, watching other kids laugh, run, and play. You want to join them, but you don’t know how. So you do what every child does: You adapt.

You laugh at jokes you don't understand. You play games you don't enjoy. You hide the parts of yourself that might make them laugh *at* you instead of *with* you.

For 12-year-old Sam, this paradox was a daily battle. *"I loved reading, but the other kids thought it was 'weird,'" he says. "So I stopped bringing books to school. I'd pretend to care about soccer, even though I hated it. I just wanted to belong. But the more I changed, the lonelier I felt."

The cost of fitting in: Every time you abandon yourself to belong, you plant another seed of loneliness. Over time, those seeds grow into forests—thick, dark, and impossible to navigate.

The Empty Room: When Punishment Feels Like Abandonment

Then there's the loneliness no one talks about: the kind that comes from being grounded. You're sitting in your room, staring at the walls, replaying the fight with your parents. *"They don't understand me,"* you think. *"They don't love me."*

But here's the truth: They do. They're trying to teach you that actions have consequences. But without explanation, without connection, the lesson gets lost. All you feel is the void.

For 15-year-old Mia, this void became a chasm. "My parents would ground me and leave me alone for hours," she says. "I'd sit there, hating them, hating myself, and feeling like the worst person in the world. I didn't learn not to make mistakes. I just learned not to get caught."

The power of a hug: Research shows that children who receive explanations and affection after being disciplined are more likely to internalize the lesson—and less likely to feel abandoned. A simple "I love you, but what you did was wrong" can bridge the gap between punishment and connection.

The Departure: When Loneliness Drives You Away

As you grow older, the seeds planted in childhood bear fruit. You start to pull away from your family, convinced they don't understand you. You build walls, not because you want to, but because you've learned that vulnerability leads to pain.

For 28-year-old Daniel, this departure was gradual but devastating. “I stopped telling my parents anything real,” he says. “I’d give them the highlights—my job, my hobbies, my plans—but I kept the hard stuff to myself. I thought I was protecting myself. But really, I was just deepening the loneliness.”

The cycle of disconnection: The less you share, the less they know you. The less they know you, the less you feel understood. And the less you feel understood, the less you share.

A Message to the Child Inside You

If you’re reading this and seeing yourself in these words, know this: You are not alone. The loneliness you feel is not your fault. It’s a wound, yes, but wounds can heal.

And if you’re a parent reading this, know this: Your child doesn’t need perfection. They need presence. They need explanations. They need hugs. They need to know that even when they mess up, they’re still loved.

A Glimmer in the Darkness

But this isn't the end. It's a turning point.

Loneliness may have shaped you, but it doesn't define you. The child who cried in the crib, the kid who hid on the playground, the teen who sat in the empty room—they're still part of you. But they don't have to control you.

The roots of loneliness run deep. But so do the roots of love.

Chapter 13

The Architect of Your Loneliness

How You Built the Walls Around Yourself

The Day You Built Your First Castle

Close your eyes and think back. When was the first time you escaped into your imagination? Maybe it was during a fight between your parents, when you hid under the covers and pretended you were in a magical forest. Maybe it was after a bad day at school, when you daydreamed about being a hero everyone adored. Or maybe it was last night, when you scrolled through

Instagram and imagined a life where you were thinner, richer, happier.

This is loneliness's greatest trick: It doesn't just isolate you from others. It isolates you from yourself.

This chapter isn't about blaming you. It's about understanding how you became the architect of your own loneliness—and how you can tear down the walls you built.

The World Inside Your Head: When Imagination Becomes a Prison

Loneliness isn't just an emotion. It's a personality—a world you create to escape the one you're in. You fill it with the music you listen to, the books you read, the movies you watch, and the stories you tell yourself. It's a place where you're loved, admired, and understood. But here's the catch: It's not real.

For 26-year-old Emma, this world became an addiction. "I'd spend hours imagining a life where I was this confident, successful version of myself," she says. "But every time I came back to reality, it felt like a slap in the face. The gap between who I was and who I wanted to be just made me lonelier."

The science of escapism: Studies show that excessive daydreaming—known as maladaptive dreaming—can worsen feelings of loneliness and depression. The more time you spend in your head, the less you engage with the world around you.

Your imagination isn't the problem. It's the *attachment* to it.

The Stargazer's Dilemma: When Loneliness Feels Like Home

Have you ever felt that the world in your imagination was better than the real world? Have you ever wished you could disappear into it?

Bingo. That's loneliness unveiled.

For 19-year-old Alex, this dilemma became a way of life. "I'd listen to sad songs and imagine this tragic love story where I was the heartbroken hero," he says. "It felt comforting, like I was the star of my own movie. But the more I stayed in that world, the harder it was to connect with real people. I didn't want a real relationship. I wanted the one in my head."

The cost of stargazing: When you romanticize loneliness, it becomes a self-fulfilling prophecy. You push people away because they don't match the fantasy—and the fantasy becomes your only companion.

The Contagion: How Loneliness Spreads

But loneliness isn't just something you create. It's something you catch.

Think about it: That friend who's always complaining about their exams. The coworker who vents about their toxic boss. The news anchor who delivers one tragic story after another. The breakup song that makes you cry even though you're not heartbroken.

You're like a sponge, absorbing the energy of everyone and everything around you. And when that energy is negative, it feeds the monster inside you.

For 33-year-old Sara, this contagion was almost unbearable. "I had a friend who was always negative," she says. “Every conversation was about how hard her life was. I’d leave her house feeling drained, like her problems were now mine. I started avoiding her, but the damage was done. I’d caught her loneliness.”

The science of emotional contagion: Research shows that emotions—especially negative ones—are contagious. Just being around someone who’s lonely or depressed can increase your own feelings of isolation.

Sympathy: The Wolf in Sheep’s Clothing

Here’s the twist: Even kindness can feed loneliness. When you sympathize with someone’s pain, you absorb it. You want them to feel better, but you don’t want to feel what they’re feeling.

For 29-year-old Jake, this realization was a wake-up call. “I’d listen to my friends vent for hours,” he says. “I thought I was being a good friend. But afterward, I’d replay their words in my head, feeling their pain as if it were my own. I didn’t realize I was carrying their loneliness until it became mine.”

The line between empathy and absorption: It's okay to care. It's okay to listen. But it's not okay to let someone else's pain become your prison.

A Glimmer in the Darkness
But this isn't the end. It's a reckoning.

You built the walls. You caught the contagion. But you can also tear it all down.

Chapter 14

The Pressure to Belong

How Jealousy and Peer Pressure Create Self-Made Loneliness

The Day You Sold Yourself for Approval

Picture this: You're sitting at lunch, watching the "it" couple at school. They're laughing, holding hands, and soaking up the attention of everyone around them. You don't even like them that much—they're shallow, dramatic, and always fighting. But still, you feel it: that pang of jealousy. That voice in your head whispering, "Why can't that be me?"

So, you do what you think you have to do. You lower your standards. You ignore your values. You chase after someone—anyone—just so you can say you're not alone.

This is loneliness's most insidious form: the kind you create yourself, not because you want to, but because you're desperate to belong.

This chapter isn't about judging you. It's about understanding how jealousy and peer pressure twist your desires—and how to break free from the cycle.

The Jealousy Trap: When You Want What You Don't Even Like

Jealousy is a liar. It convinces you that someone else's life is better than yours—even when it's not.

For 17-year-old Mia, this trap was almost inescapable. “There was this girl in my class who always had a boyfriend,” she says.

“They were never good guys, and she was always crying over them. But I still wanted what she had. I thought having a boyfriend would make me popular, like her. So, I started dating this guy I didn’t even like. He was rude, possessive, and made me feel awful about myself. But I stayed with him because I didn’t want to be alone.”

The cost of comparison: When you chase someone else’s life, you abandon your own. You trade your values for validation, your self-respect for attention, and your happiness for a facade.

The Peer Pressure Paradox: When Friendship Feels Like a Test

Peer pressure doesn’t always come in the form of “Just try it!” Sometimes, it’s subtler. It’s the way your friends talk about their relationships, their hookups, their adventures. It’s the way they look at you when you say you're not interested. It's the way they make you feel like you're missing out.

For 20-year-old Jake, this paradox cost him his self-respect. "My friends were always pressuring me to lose my virginity," he says. *"They'd say things like, *'You're not a man until you've done it.' So, I hooked up with someone I barely knew. I didn't even want to, but I didn't want to be the odd one out. Afterward, I felt empty. I didn't feel like a man. I felt like a fraud."

The science of conformity: Studies show that peer pressure activates the brain's reward system, making you more likely to conform—even when it goes against your values. The fear of rejection is stronger than the fear of regret.

The Self-Born Loneliness: When You Betray Yourself
Here's the hardest truth: The loneliness you feel after giving in to jealousy or peer pressure isn't caused by others. It's caused by you.

Every time you lower your standards, ignore your instincts, or betray your values, you chip away at your self-worth. You become a stranger to yourself—someone you don't recognize, someone you don't even like.

For 22-year-old Priya, this self-betrayal was a wake-up call. *"I dated this guy because all my friends thought he was hot,"she says. "But he was toxic. He'd put me down in front of them, and I'd just laugh it off because I didn't want to seem 'difficult.' One day, I looked in the mirror and didn't recognize myself. I was so busy trying to be what everyone else wanted, I forgot who I was."

The anatomy of self-betrayal:

1. Comparison: You see someone else's life and think it's better than yours.
2. Conformity: You change yourself to fit in, even if it goes against your values.
3. Collapse: You feel lonelier than ever because you've abandoned yourself.

The Question You Need to Ask Yourself

Why are you chasing a life you don't even want?

Is it because you're jealous? Because you're afraid of being left out? Because you think you're not enough as you are?

Whatever the reason, it's time to stop.

A Glimmer in the Darkness

But this isn't the end. It's a turning point.

You don't have to live someone else's life. You don't have to betray yourself to belong. You don't have to let jealousy or peer pressure dictate your choices.

—----------

Chapter 15

The Academic Arena.

How Grades, Envy, and Jealousy Breed Loneliness

You're sitting in class, waiting for the teacher to hand back the exams. Your stomach churns as you imagine the possibilities: Did you pass? Did you fail? Did you do better than them? When the paper lands on your desk, you don't even look at your grade first. You glance sideways, scanning your classmates' scores. Relief floods you if you did better. Shame burns if you didn't. This is the academic arena—a battlefield where grades aren't just numbers. They're weapons. They're status symbols. They're the measure of your worth.

This chapter isn't about studying harder. It's about understanding how the pressure to perform, the envy of others, and the jealousy within you create a loneliness that no grade can cure.

If you've ever failed a test, you know the sting of judgment. The teacher's disappointed sigh. The classmates' whispered comments. The sinking feeling that you're not smart enough, not good enough, not enough. For 16-year-old Sam, this hostility was crushing. "I failed a math test, and my teacher called me out in front of the whole class," he says. "Everyone laughed, but I wanted to disappear. After that, I stopped raising my hand, stopped asking questions, stopped trying. I felt like I didn't belong in that classroom—or anywhere." When grades define your worth, failure doesn't just hurt your GPA. It hurts your sense of belonging. You start to see yourself as an outsider, unworthy of connection.

But here's the twist: Even success can breed loneliness. For 18-year-old Aisha, being at the top of her class was isolating. “My friends would joke about how I was the ‘smart one,’ but it didn’t feel like a compliment,” she says. “They’d exclude me from study groups, saying I didn’t need the help. When I aced a test, they’d roll their eyes or make snide comments. I thought being the best would make me feel proud. Instead, it made me feel alone.” The higher you climb, the lonelier it gets. Your achievements become a barrier, separating you from the people you care about.

Every friendship group has its hierarchies. The “smart one.” The “funny one.” The “popular one.” But when those roles are tied to academic performance, the cracks start to show. For 15-year-old Jake, this fracture was devastating. “My best friend and I used to do everything together,” he says. “But when I started getting better grades than him, things changed. He’d make passive-aggressive comments, like, ‘Must be nice to be a genius.’ I tried to downplay my success, but it didn’t help. Eventually, we stopped talking. I lost my best friend—and it was all because of grades.” Envy—especially among friends—can destroy relationships. When you feel threatened by someone’s success, you either pull away or try to tear them down. Either way, the connection is lost.

Here's the hardest truth: The loneliness you feel isn't just caused by others. It's caused by you. How many times have you tried to outshine a friend, not because you wanted to succeed, but because you wanted to *beat them*? How many times have you hidden your struggles, not because you were fine, but because you didn't want to seem weak? For 17-year-old Mia, this cycle was exhausting. "I was always comparing myself to my friends," she says. "If they got a better grade, I'd feel like a failure. If I got a better grade, I'd feel guilty. I couldn't win. No matter what I did, I felt alone."

Why are you competing with the people who are supposed to be on your team? Is it because you're afraid of being left behind? Because you think your worth is tied to your grades? Because you've forgotten that success isn't a zero-sum game? Whatever the reason, it's time to stop.

Grades don't define you. Envy doesn't control you. Jealousy doesn't own you. You are more than your GPA, more than your rank, more than your achievements. In the next chapter, we'll explore **The Liberation**: how to break free from the academic arena, rebuild friendships without competition, and find joy in learning—not just in winning. You'll meet a student who quit the rat race to rediscover her passion, a teacher who transformed her classroom into a community, and a group of friends who learned to celebrate each other's successes without envy.

The grades you chase aren't the ones that matter. The ones that matter are the ones you give yourself: for kindness, for courage, for being authentically you. Turn the page. Start living for more than a score.

Chapter 16

The Liberation

Breaking Free from the Academic Arena

You've spent years in the academic arena, fighting for grades, scrambling for approval, and measuring your worth by numbers on a page. But what if the arena isn't the only stage? What if there's a world beyond the rankings, the envy, and the endless competition? A world where learning is joyful, friendships are genuine, and success isn't a zero-sum game?

This chapter is about liberation—about breaking free from the chains of academic pressure and rediscovering what it means to learn, to connect, and to thrive. It's about the student who quit the rat race, the teacher who redefined her classroom, and the friends who learned to celebrate each other without envy.

The Student Who Quit the Rat Race

Meet 19-year-old Priya, a straight-A student who had it all: top grades, a scholarship to a prestigious university, and a future that looked like a blueprint for success. But beneath the surface, she was drowning.

"I was so focused on being the best that I forgot why I even started," she says. "I stopped reading for fun because it didn't 'count.' I stopped hanging out with friends because I needed to study. I even stopped sleeping because I was so scared of falling behind. One day, I looked in the mirror and didn't recognize myself. I was a machine, not a person."

Priya's breaking point came during her second year of university. She was preparing for a midterm when she realized she couldn't remember the last time she'd felt happy. "I was sitting in the library, surrounded by books, and I just started crying. I thought, 'What's the point of all this if I'm miserable?"

That day, Priya made a radical decision: She dropped out. Not because she didn't care about her future, but because she cared about herself. "I needed to remember who I was outside of grades and expectations," she says.

Priya spent the next year traveling, volunteering, and rediscovering her love of learning. She read books that weren't on any syllabus. She took classes that didn't come with grades. She even started a blog about her journey, which unexpectedly went viral.

"I thought quitting would ruin my life," she says. "But it saved me. I realized that success isn't about being the best. It's about being you."

The Teacher Who Transformed Her Classroom

Ms. Carter had been teaching high school English for over a decade when she noticed something troubling: Her students were more stressed than ever. "They weren't learning for the joy of it," she says. "They were learning to survive."

Determined to change the culture, Ms. Carter introduced a radical experiment: a grade-free semester. “I told my students, ‘This isn’t about scores. It’s about growth. Let’s focus on curiosity, creativity, and connection.’”

At first, her students were skeptical. “We thought it was a trick,” says 16-year-old Marcus. “But then we realized she was serious. For the first time, I felt like I could breathe.”

Without the pressure of grades, the classroom transformed. Students who had been silent started sharing their ideas. Projects became collaborations, not competitions. Even the “slackers” started showing up—not because they had to, but because they wanted to.

“It wasn’t perfect,” Ms. Carter admits. “Some kids struggled with the lack of structure. But overall, it was a revelation. They weren’t just learning. They were *living.*”

The Friends Who Celebrated Each Other

For 17-year-old Emma, friendship had always been a competition. “We were always comparing ourselves—grades, looks, boyfriends,” she says. “It was exhausting.”

Everything changed when Emma’s best friend, Sarah, got into her dream college. “I was happy for her, but I also felt this pang of jealousy,” Emma admits. “I thought, ‘Why her and not me?”

Instead of hiding her feelings, Emma decided to be honest. “I told Sarah how I felt,” she says. “And you know what? She understood. She said, ‘I’ve felt the same way about you.”

That conversation sparked a new way of relating. Emma and Sarah made a pact: No more comparisons. No more envy. Just support. “We started celebrating each other’s wins, no matter how small,” Emma says. “If she aced a test, I’d take her out for ice cream. If I got a part in the school play, she’d be in the front row cheering. It changed everything.”

Their friendship became a model for their entire group. “We realized that there’s enough success to go around," Emma says. "When one of us wins, we all win."

The Liberation: How to Break Free

Priya, Ms. Carter, and Emma's stories show that liberation is possible—but it requires courage, creativity, and a willingness to let go of old ways of thinking. Here's how you can start:

1. Redefine Success: Ask yourself, "What does success mean to me?" Is it about grades, or is it about growth? Is it about being the best, or is it about being *you*?

2. Celebrate Collaboration: Instead of competing with your peers, collaborate with them. Study together. Share ideas. Celebrate each other's wins.

3. Focus on Joy: Rediscover the joy of learning. Read a book just because it interests you. Take a class just because it excites you. Let curiosity, not pressure, guide you.

4. Be Honest About Envy: When you feel jealous, don't hide it. Acknowledge it. Talk about it. You might be surprised by how much others relate.

5. Create a Support System: Surround yourself with people who celebrate you, not compete with you. Build friendships based on trust, not comparison.

A Glimmer in the Darkness

The academic arena doesn't have to be a battlefield. It can be a playground—a place to explore, to grow, to connect. The grades you chase aren't the ones that matter. The ones that matter are the ones you give yourself: for kindness, for courage, for being authentically you.

Turn the page. Start living for more than a score.

————

Chapter 17

The Anatomy of Loneliness

How to Heal the Wounds and Reclaim Your Life

Loneliness isn't a single beast. It's a hydra monster that grows new heads every time you cut one off. It's the ache of being unseen as a child, the pressure to fit in as a teen, the envy of others' success, the masks you wear to belong, and the worlds you create in your head to escape. But here's the truth: Loneliness isn't your fault. It's a wound that society, relationships, and even you have inflicted. And like any wound, it can heal.

Let's revisit the roots of this beast. It begins in the crib, where the seeds of loneliness are planted when your needs aren't met consistently, leaving you with a fear of abandonment. It grows on the playground, where the pressure to fit in forces you to abandon your true self, creating a cycle of performance and isolation. It thrives in the academic arena, where envy and competition fracture friendships and make success feel like a lonely climb. It festers behind the masks you wear, the people-pleasing personas that disconnect you from your authentic self and the people who truly care about you. It hides in the world inside your head, where escapism turns your imagination into a prison, making reality feel unbearable. It spreads like a contagion, feeding on the negative energy you absorb from others. And it tightens its grip through the pressure to belong, the jealousy and peer pressure that lead you to betray your values and abandon your self-worth.

Each of these roots feeds the beast, but each also holds a key to its defeat. Healing loneliness isn't about quick fixes or superficial solutions. It's about addressing the roots—the wounds, the patterns, the lies you've internalized.

Start by reconnecting with your inner child. That lonely child inside you is still there, waiting to be seen and heard. Spend time reflecting on your early experiences of loneliness. What did you need then that you didn't get? How can you give it to yourself now? Try writing a letter to your younger self. Tell them they're loved, they're enough, and they don't have to earn belonging.

Next, tear off the masks. You don't have to perform to be loved. Start small: Share an unpopular opinion. Say no to something you don't want to do. Let someone see the real you, even if it's messy. Identify one mask you wear regularly, the "perfect" friend, the "easygoing" coworker and practice taking it off in safe spaces.

Break the cycle of comparison. Grades, looks, relationships none of these define your worth. Celebrate your successes without comparing them to others'. Celebrate others' successes without feeling threatened. The next time you feel envy, reframe it. Instead of thinking, "Why don't I have that?" ask, "What can I learn from them?"

Set boundaries with negative energy. You don't have to absorb everyone else's pain. Listen with empathy, but don't take on their loneliness as your own. Protect your energy like it's your most precious resource because it is. After a draining conversation, take five minutes to ground yourself. Breathe deeply, visualize releasing the negative energy, and remind yourself of your own worth.

Reclaim your imagination. Your imagination is a gift, not a prison. Use it to create, not escape. Write stories, paint, dream big but always come back to the real world, where true connection lives. Spend 10 minutes each day journaling about your real-life goals and dreams. How can you take one small step toward them today?

Rebuild authentic connections. Loneliness thrives in isolation, but it withers in connection. Reach out to someone you trust. Share something real. Let them see the cracks in your armor that's where the light gets in. Text a friend or family member and say, "I've been feeling lonely lately. Can we talk?"

Finally, practice self-compassion. You are not your mistakes, your failures, or your loneliness. You are a human being, worthy of love and belonging just as you are. When you catch yourself being self-critical, ask, "Would I say this to someone I love?" If the answer is no, don't say it to yourself.

What would your life look like if you stopped running from loneliness and started facing it? What if, instead of hiding, you showed up as you are, not as you think you should be? What if, instead of competing, you connected? What if, instead of escaping, you embraced the messy, beautiful reality of being human?

Loneliness is a wound, but it's also a teacher. It shows you where you've abandoned yourself, where you've disconnected from others, and where you've bought into society's lies. Healing isn't easy. It's a journey one that requires courage, vulnerability, and patience. But it's also a journey worth taking. Because on the other side of loneliness is connection. On the other side of pain is joy. On the other side of the mask is you.

Turn the page. Start healing. The world needs the real you not the mask, not the performance, not the fantasy. Just you.

Think of one small step you can take today to heal your loneliness. What's one way you can show up authentically, set a boundary, or reconnect with someone you care about? The journey begins with a single step. Take it.

References

—-----------

special thank you to all the people who allowed me to interview them and study their mental health. Thank you to all my clients for allowing me to conduct mental studies on them and allowing me to reference them in my book and to all the wonderful schools who allowed me to conduct my observations and interviews at their school. Thank you to the couples who allowed me to observe their children's behaviour and to all the people who helped me conduct my study.

Thank you to my clients
Sarah, Mark , Jamie , Dev and Elena for being wonderful and encouraging clients and allowing me to conduct my studies on them.
Thanks to my friends Lila Willson, Marcus woo, Ryan Wondom, Sam Francis, Priya Marson and Maria Lee.

Thanks to the teachers that I cannot mention their names due to privacy and integrity reasons.

Thanks to the couples Nina and Amir young, Sofia and Carlos brown, Mia and James woolen, Emma and Alex salavinsi and Sara and Jake wellson.
A sweet Thank you to my dear mother who was my moral support and source of comfort and to all my siblings for being there for me when I couldn't complete my book and to all the people who took time out of their schedules to be a part of this book. Thank you so much for your hard work and contribution.

www.ingramcontent.com/pod-product-compliance
Lightning Source LLC
LaVergne TN
LVHW060043210926
848481LV00013B/3944